Panorama of
German Life

Alfred Lau

Panorama of German Life

Deutschland wie es lebt

Univers-Verlag
Bielefeld

Erschienen: Publisher:	im Univers-Verlag, 4. verbesserte Auflage Univers-Verlag, 4rd edition
Herausgeber: Editor:	Alfred Lau
Management:	Ralph Plum, Heide Ringhand
Fotos: Photographs:	Aero-Lux, Antonoff, Baumann, Bormann, Brenker, Central-Color, Cornelius, Deak, Expression, Feininger, Fischer, Gauls, Gering, Gierig, Groth- Schmachtenberg, Gunkel, Halbach, Hanisch, Harz, Hauswald und Heckenroth, Hehl, Hensel, Herford, Hetz, Holcomb, Höpcker, Huber, Jorde, Kaster, Keetmann, Klammet, Knopf, Kratochwil, Krug, LAD, Lau, Lelanz, Löbl, Meyer, Moog, Mollenhauer, Munker, Nieswandt, Reimann, Rossenbach, Dr. Schiffer, Schneiders, UHB, Werek, Dr. Wolff & Tritschler und Archiv-Fotos
Text:	Horst Hachmann
Gestaltung: Design:	Albrecht Ade, Alfred Lau
Übersetzungen: Translations:	ADINTRA All Language Services, Brüssel, Gisela Hack, Bonn-Bad Godesberg, Expert-Team, Düsseldorf
Gesamtherstellung: Printer:	Universitätsdruckerei H. Stürtz AG, Würzburg

Luftbildfreigabe:
Die einzelnen Luftbilder in diesem Band wurden wie folgt freigegeben:

Rechberg	– durch Regierung von Oberbayern	Nr. G 43/750
Karlsruhe	– durch Reg.-Präsidium Nord-Württemberg	Nr. 2/32597 C
Bremen	– durch Senator für Häfen, Schiffahrt und Verkehr der Freien Hansestadt Bremen	Nr. FE 72–0809/2
Schloß Burg	– durch Reg.-Präsidium Düsseldorf	Nr. 19/32/3070
Passau	– durch Regierung von Oberbayern	Nr. G 43/221
Alpen	– durch Regierung von Oberbayern	Nr. G 43/797
Duisburg	– durch Reg.-Präsidium Düsseldorf	So Nr. 18/2442
Weser- Mündung	– beim Senator für Häfen, Schiffahrt und Verkehr Bremen	Nr. FE 72/0713–43
Stadion Düsseldorf	– durch Reg.-Präsidium Düsseldorf	Nr. 19/C 552

The Triumph of Diversity

If you ask a stranger what comes into his mind when he hears "The Federal Republic of Germany", he will have at least a dozen answers ready. He will mention the Volkswagen and the Autobahn. Berlin and Kurfürstendamm will be on his list, together with Munich and its Hofbräuhaus and of course the industrial landscape of the Rhine and Ruhr. The catchword "Romanticism" will occur to him, and perhaps Goethe and Beethoven. In any event he will think of citadels, castles and Cathedrals, and of Heidelberg. For him Germany is also plates of Sauerkraut, miniature gardens and nudist beaches, giant breweries, a workshop for luxury cars and a Lederhosen factory.

This is no random list. Public opinion pollsters have set it up, as they endeavoured to reconstruct the image of the Federal Republic abroad. What came out of it is a catalogue of snapshots. If one puts them together they will show a few outlines, but one cannot combine them into a portrait. For this one needs a few hundred themes and a loving eye for detail. The passing visitor can only turn towards each item of value that is offered to him in our great cities, as it were out of the samples case of a commercial traveller. Chrome-plated cars in the street, bulging shop windows, international cuisine and neon lights glistening through the night show him wealth and well-being. He lets himself be mesmerised by the glitter of the superficial. The picture that bewitches him, and which he sees forever reproduced in the media, is but a pebble in the scintillating mosaic called Germany.

This volume traces many outlines. Renowned photographers have illustrated the imperishable as well as the transient. Cities and countryside, industry and trade, people and leisure, culture, tradition and progress make up the technical background of this big, colourful report.

Germany, our country, is divided as the result of a national disaster which brought about the emergence of two States on German soil. In Germany's history, 23rd May 1949 stands out as the birthday of the Federal Republic. On that day the Basic Law was promulgated, one of the most liberal constitutions the world knows. In Bonn, which was then declared the provisional capital, the state organs were constituted in September 1949 – Bundestag, Bundesrat, Federal President and Federal Government.

Since this "Year One" of our contemporary history, there has been going on in our country a building-up process which is unprecedented and is called a "miracle" throughout the world. But any dispassionate assessment of our present position, in the great procession of the world's peoples, must begin with the judgment that this miracle was only possible thanks to the tolerance and the will to reconciliation of our former enemies in the western world, with whom we are linked today in a close and friendly association. We all, the 60 million citizens of this country, are shareholders in this democratic enterprise called the Federal Republic. Our social compact, that is the Basic Law, ensures us the fullest rights. It guarantees our human dignity and confirms by charter the right to free development of the personality and to equality before the law. It underwrites freedom of religious belief and affiliation, the right to express our opinions freely, freedom of assembly, freedom of association and complete freedom of movement. Marriage and the family are protected along with the inviolability of home and of property, and no man can restrict our free choice of trade or profession.

We also have a voice in our "concern". This is once again specified in Article 20, which expressly states "all political power comes from the people." We are therefore sovereign, we express our will directly through the Bundestag elections. In other words – the head of our firm is governed by our will. To ensure this remains the case, the fathers of our constitution have built in a reassuring brake. Anyone who misuses our basic rights in order to fight against democracy, thereby infringes them.

Friends from abroad and a moderate policy, continually developing from the fruitful inter-play of our parliamentary life, have helped the "Federal Republic Enterprise" to achieve world status. The factory chimneys smoke, the cars roll on, and middle-class satisfaction reigns in the home. We can show our country with confidence. Foreign visitors gladly come to us again. For the rumour has spread around the world: the Federal Republic is worth seeing.

Whoever travels through our country, from North to South, lives through a tourist gala performance, with continually changing scenery. Sea and sandbank, and with luck even a windmill, cars in convoy on a fast road and a horse trudging along the meadow-path. Then pasture spreading like an endless carpet and upon it, as though arranged for an idyllic tryst, cuddly sheep that seem to come from an advertising photograph. Then, suddenly, there appears a lake or a wood or a hill. Rivers, with dazzling white ships on them. And a church in the midst of vineyards, many timber-framed houses in romantic little towns, the sound of cow bells on mountain pastures, students arguing in a market place. In Germany, diversity reigns. Every thirty miles the countryside takes on another aspect, as if a skilled scene-setter had a hand in the play.

Nor is it otherwise with our cities and towns. There are exactly 1374 of them – enough to take one's pick. Many are ultra-modern; many breathe out tradition in every timber beam. But no two are alike, and all have their landmarks. The glass-and-concrete architecture of our time leaves room enough for the imperishable signposts of our history: cathedrals and churches stand like models from the construction sets of a past age; weighty, compact Romanesque, lofty Gothic, splendid Baroque. Around them, here and there, city walls remain, overgrown with the moss of centuries.

Cities, like giant stage scenes. Everyday life writes the script: sometimes a mystery play, sometimes comedy, sometimes drama, sometimes operetta and now and then crime fiction. It follows a set programme round the clock: work, live, love, laugh, play, discuss.

And what of the German, who puts on this show, the often caricatured Michael with his night-cap? Now – he is 5ft 7 tall, earns 2525 mark gross a month, drinks 21 gallons of beer a year, brings up two children, sees his car as his most precious possession and goes once a week to play skittles or drink in his favourite bar.

As a creature standardised along those lines on a single pattern, he has worked the miracle, with all mankind looking on, of steering Germany back into the ranks of the world's ten major industrial states, after the uttermost of all defeats. But this standard German is fortunately no more than a statistical figure-head serving the national image. To him must be added men who make a unique contribution, and make it afresh every day: the harbour pilot, who safely guides the ocean giants to their dock, the miner, bringing coal out from the hillside, the scientist, who in the loneliness of the Eifel sends messages out into other social systems, the farmer, the factory worker, the railwayman, the teacher.

The environment, or as one calls it with pathos, the homeland, has made its mark upon them all. Language and way of life give proof of this. Nuances indicate the differences. Nuances in the way people laugh, in their gestures. In the North the table is not laid out in the same way as in the South. And the Friesian lass from the Emsland is as different from the Bavarian Dirndl as the sea from the mountains. The wine-grower from the banks of the Mosel speaks and moves otherwise than the Stuttgart car worker. Yet distinctions are no longer as clear as they were 50 years ago. The great postwar migrations have blurred regional differences. And the industrial society, which moves people around like pieces on a chessboard, hastens this process of assimilation.

The journey back into our past with the time-machine is like a historical wide-screen film, breath-taking in its drama. Outstanding producers have worked on the script. Only a few names and stations have been recorded on the time-accelerator: Charlemagne and the "Holy Roman Empire of the German Nation", with the solid development of Europe's heartland. Then the break-up of the Empire and the rule of princes. Luther and the Reformation are milestones at the same time in our cultural and in our linguistic development. Social and economic tensions build up the powder-keg og the Peasants' War. The Thirty Years' War fails to resolve our religious divisions, but leaves behind a trail of scorched earth, poverty, hunger and pestilence.

At a time of political impotence culture becomes the great landmark. The age of Classicism and Romanticism brings mighty names to the fore: Klopstock and Lessing, Hegel and Kant, Goethe and Schiller, Humboldt and Schleiermacher, Beethoven. Europe calls us "The land of poets and philosophers". Prussia becomes one of the dominant stations of the journey through time: Frederick the Great creates a major power and alters the political system: Napoleon marches on to the stage and changes the German scenery again. The Confederation of the Rhine replaces the Holy Roman Empire of the German Nation: 1848 sees the failure of the attempt to establish a united Germany. The age of middle-class supremacy opens with rebellion, with Karl Marx and Friedrich Engels. In 1871 Germany achieves national unity at last. The chancellor is called Bismarck: ten years later we have a hitherto unique system of social legislation. At the same time the great inventors make their impact: Gottlieb Daimler, Heinrich Hertz, Wilhelm Röntgen, Albert Einstein.

The aftermath of the first great defeat leads the state to inflation, unrest and the verge of chaos. At the same time Berlin becomes the centre of the "Golden Twenties". The Bauhaus in Weimar with Kardinsky, Klee and Gropius sets the tone of modern art and architecture. Unemployment leads to radicalism. Depression and want finally bring Hitler to power as dictator, and the weak are driven to the wall. National megalomania and the overthrow of the basic rights of liberal democracy lead Germany to the abyss. But even through this recent past we can understand why the people of the Federal Republic are proud of their State today. For there is scarce one generation to whom history has not bequeathed a heap of ruins, but never was the chaos more complete than in 1945. In that hour of deepest national darkness, the will to survive asserted itself.

Concrete and Glass, Patina and Romanticism Galore

The Federal Republic is a prospectus of towns with exactly 1374 entries. With metropoles and dormitory towns; with fair cities and congress centres, Hanseatic and university cities, industrial towns and resorts. The largest has two million inhabitants: the smallest has fewer than 500. Many are ultra-modern, while in others it is only the television aerials on the roofs that remind us we are living in the 20th Century. Not one of them looks like the rest. All have their own characteristic relationship with the countryside.
Many names speak to us of tradition and progress, of trade and traffic, of history and culture, and of the great men who have gone before us. Dürer stands for Nuremberg, Beethoven for Bonn, Goethe for Frankfurt and Gutenberg for Mainz.

The cities are as ever the brilliant backdrop for an unprecedented tourist display. The matter-of-factness of modern functional buildings stands in harmonious contrast with the past: concrete-and-glass beside picturesque timber-framed houses, prefabricated buildings next to ornate towers and heavy gates, glistening aluminium alongside patina domes. And in whatever city one may stop, it is always only a short distance to one of the typical German holiday areas.

In Cologne, Dusseldorf or Bonn, German Romanticism stands before the front door. The great Rhine cruise is considered a must for visitors from overseas, who would like to experience at first hand the charm of the German citadels. Kunegunde, the lady of the castle, lays the table with decorum: the Lorelei legends and the Drosselgasse trumpets remain until now irreplaceable assets in the balance-sheet of German travel. This by the way, is also true of Heidelberg, where one can now observe the students demonstrating as well as drinking beer. Yet Gaudeamus Igitur resounds as lustily as ever.

In Rothenburg above the Tauber, this miniature town of timber frames and perfect cuisine, the "Fairy Tale Book of Germany" has opened at its most enchanting page. Here one is even now in the midst of the purest Middle Ages. And if he has made his way that far south, the globetrotter must also "tick off" the royal castles of the Füssen Fore-Alps, whose pomp and splendour have won immortality for King Ludwig of Bavaria and have given the countryside one of the most famous starred entries in Baedeker.

Frankfurt is the central starting point for excursions throughout Germany. Here, on the turntable of Germany, with the international Rhine-Main airport was not only the home of Goethe, the prince of poets, whose parents' house is a stopping-place for several dozen tourist coaches day after day; here, with the broad rotunda of the Pauluskirche, stands the cradle of German democracy. People say Frankfurt is the most American of our great cities. It is also the most international and cosmopolitan. From Frankfurt one can cover Germany in a few hours: an hour's flight away is Berlin, the divided former capital. The Kurfurstendamm, the main artery of the city, is even now one of the greatest promenades in Europe.

(continued on page 65)

Festbeleuchtung für Kaiserburg und Pilatus-Haus, Nürnberg

Festive illumination for Kaiserburg and Pilatus-Haus in Nuremberg

Illuminations de fête pour le chateau royal et la maison de Pilatus â Nurenberg

Iluminación de fiesta para el "Kaiserburg" (castillo del emperador)

Alpen-Panorama

The Alps

Panorama alpin

Panorama de los Alpes

Die „Rote Insel":
Blick auf Helgoland

Heligoland, the
"Red Island"

L'«Ile rouge»: vue de
Helgoland

La "Isla Roja": vista
hacia Helgoland

< Schwäbische Alb mit
Burgruine Rechberg

Swabian Jura and the
ruins of Rechberg castle

Le Jura souabe
(«Schwäbische Alb»)
avec les ruines du
château fort de Rechberg

Schwäbische Alb con las

ruinas del castillo de
Rechberg

Segel-Wettbewerbe
bei der „Kieler Woche"

Sailing competition
during the "Kieler
Woche"

Régate de voiliers
à l'occasion de la
«Semaine de Kiel»
(Kieler Woche)

Regata de veleros
durante la "Semana
de Kiel"

Saarbrücken aus der
Luft gesehen
_____

Aerial view
of Saarbrücken

Vue áerinne de
Sarrebruck
_____

Saarbrücken visto
desde el aire

Blick von der Sparren-
burg über Bielefeld
_____

View of the Sparrenburg
near Bielefeld

Du château
«Sparrenburg», le regard
embrasse la ville de
Bielefeld
_____

Vista desde el castillo
de Sparrenburg sobre
Bielefeld

Feuerwerk über
Frankfurt, der
Metropole am Main

Fireworks over
Frankfurt, the
metropolis on the river
Main
_____
Feu d'artifice sur
Francfort, la métropole
sur le Main

Fuegos Artificiales
sobre Francfort del
Meno

Das Heidelberger Schloß
_____
Heidelberg castle
_____
Le château de Heidelberg
_____
Castillo de Heidelberg

Das Bergbaumuseum in Bochum – täglich Ziel vieler Besucher

Bochum's Mining Museum – many visitors every day

Le musée de la mine á Bochum accueille quotidiennement un grand nombre de visiteurs

El museo minero en Bochum, podos los dias hecode muchos viestidores

Blick über das nächtliche Berlin

View of Berlin at night

Berlin vue de unit

Vista sobre Berlin en la noche

Burg Rheinstein bei Bingen
am Rhein

The castle of Rheinstein
near Bingen on the Rhine

Le château de Rheinstein
près de Bingen sur le Rhin

El castillo de Rheinstein
cerca de Bingen en el valle
del Rin

Millionenfach
fotografiert: Schloß
Neuschwanstein mit
Alpsee

Photographed a million
times: Neuschwanstein
castle

Le château de
Neuschwanstein avec
l'Alpsee

El castillo de
Neuschwanstein junto
al Alpsee

Wasserschloß Lembeck
in Dorsten (Münsterland)

The moated Lembeck
Castle in the Münsterland

Lé château entouré d'eau
de Lembeck, dans la région
de Munster

Wasserschloß Lembeck
en el Münsterland

St. Bartholomä mit
Königssee

St. Bartholomä with
the Königssee

St Bartholomé avec
le Königssee

San Bartolomé junto
al Königssee

Schönberger Strand an >
der Ostsee

Beach at Schönberg on
the Baltic

Plage de Schönberg sur
la mer Baltique

Playa de Schönberg en
el Mar Báltico

Kirche St. Michael in
Fulda (820)

St. Michael's church in
Fulda (built in 820)

Eglise St. Michel à
Fulda (bâtie en 820)

Iglesia de San Miguel
en Fulda, construida
en el 820

Moderner
„Fels des Glaubens" –
Wallfahrtskirche in
Velbert/Neviges

Modern "Rock of be-
lief" – the pilgrimage
church at Velbert-
Neviges

Le «Rocher de la Foi»
moderne – L'église du
lieu de pèlerinage de
Velbert/Neviges

La moderna "Roca de
la Fe" – iglesia de
peregrinación en
Velbert/Neviges

Kurmittelhaus im
Staatsbad Salzuflen

Main sanatorium
at national health resort
at Salzuflen

Firme de produits pour
cure dans la ville d'eaux
de Bad Salzuflen

El centro terapéutico
del balneario del Estado
de Salzuflen

Taunus-Therme Bad
Homburg, Gesundheits-
bad im Kurpark

Bad Homburg, a well
known spa in the Taunus
range. A view of the Kur-
park

Une station balnéaire dans
les collines du Taunus: Bad
Homburg. Vue du Kur-
park

Una estación balnearia en
las colinas del Taunus, Bad
Homburg. En el parque de
las termas

Moderne Architektur:
Verwaltungszentrum
von RWI, Düsseldorf

Modern architecture:
Administration center
of the RWI, Düsseldorf

Architecture moderne:
Le centre administratif
de la caisse d'épargne-
construction de RWI,
Düsseldorf

Arquitectura moderna:
centro de administración
de RWI, Düsseldorf

Würzburg mit Festung   >
Marienberg

The city of Würzburg with
the citadel of Marienberg

La ville de Würzburg avec
la citadelle de Marienberg

La ciudad de Würzburg
con la fortaleza de Marienberg

Verträumter Winkel in
Hattingen

A dreamy nook in Hattin-
gen

Un coin pittoresque de
Hattingen

Un rencón romantico nen
Hattingen

Wiesbaden: Kranzplatz
mit Kochbrunnentempel

Wiesbaden: Kranz square
and the "Kochbrunnen
fountain"

Wiesbaden: la place Kranz
et le «temple» de la fontaine
«Kochbrunnen»

Wiesbaden: Plaza Kranz y
el fuente "Kochbrunnen"

Freudenberg im
Siegerland

Freudenberg, Siegerland

Freudenberg dans le
Siegerland

Freudenberg en la
región de Siegerland

Jagdschloß Clemenswerth
– Barockbaukunst im Ems-
land

The hunting lodge of
Clemenswerth – a beautiful
baroque castle in the Ems
region

Le pavillon de chasse de
Clemenswerth – exemple
de l'art baroque dans la
region de l'Ems

El castillo de caza de
Clemenswerth – ejentlo del
arte barrueco en la región
de la Ems

Traditionsbeladen:
Der Dom zu Worms

Historic Worms
cathedral

Chargée du poide de
l'histoire, la Cathédrale
de Worms

Cargada de tradición:
la Catedral de Worms

Erhabenes Denkmal
abendländischer Kultur:
Der Aachener Dom

Magnificent monument
of Western culture:
The Aachen Cathedral

Imposant monument
de la civilisation occi-
dentale: La cathédrale
d'Aix-la-Chapelle

Monumento majestuoso
de cultura occidental:
la catedral de Aquisgrán

„... in dem wunder-
schönen Land."
Wilseder Berg in der
Lüneburger Heide

«Wilseder Berg»,
un mont du site protégé
de la Lande de Lüneburg
(Lüneburger Heide)

Solingens aparte „Vor-
stadt": Schloß Burg

Schloß Burg,
le «faubourg» original
de Solingen

Near the Wilseder Berg
in the Lüneburger Heide
natural reserve

Al pie del Wilseder Berg,
en el Parque Nacional
Lüneburger Heide

Solingen's striking
"suburb": Schloss Burg

El suburbio encantador
de Solingen: Schloß
Burg

Der Plenarsaal des
Deutschen Bundestages

La salle plénière du
Bundestag

The plenary assembly
hall of the German
Bundestag (Lower
House of Parliament)

La sala plenaria de del
Bundestag alemán

Modernes Verwaltungs-
gebäude der Rank
Xerox GmbH,
Düsseldorf

Rank Xerox building,
Düsseldorf

Bâtiment administratif
moderne de la Sté Rank
Xerox GmbH à
Düsseldorf

Edificio administrativo
de la Rank Xerox en
Düsseldorf

Donaudurchbruch bei
Kelheim   >

The gorge of the Danube
near Kelheim

Le défilé du Danube près
de Kelheim

El desfiladero del Danubio
derca de Kelheim

„Harmonische Kontraste": Bensberg/Bergisch Gladbach

Contrasts and harmony: the cities of Bensberg and Bergisch Gladbach

Contrastes et harmonie: Bensberg/Bergisch Gladbach

Constrastes y harmonía: Las ciudades de Bensberg y Bergisch-Gladbach

Modernes Bürgerhaus „Bergischer Löwe" in Bergisch Gladbach

A modern residence called "Bergischer Löwe" in Bergisch Gladbach

Une résidence moderne, le «Bergischer Löwe», (Lion du pays de Berg) à Bergisch Gladbach

Casa residencial moderna "Bergischer Löwe" (León del país de Berg) à Bergisch Gladbach

Das Holstentor als
Wahrzeichen der
Hansestadt Lübeck

The Holstentor,
landmark of the Hanse
Town of Lübeck

Le Holstentor comme
signe caracteristique de
la ville hanséatique
Lübeck

La puerta "Holstentor"
como monumento
característico de la

ciudad hanseática
Lübeck

Im Hamburger Hafen
mit Blick zum „Michel"

In the port at Hamburg,
looking towards the
"Michel"

Dans le port de
Hambourg: vue sur la
flèche de l'Eglise
«St Michel»

Puerto de Hamburgo
con vista hacia el
"Michel"

It is also an hour's flight, or four and a half hours by T.E.E. to Hamburg,
the metropolis of the North, the city with the biggest port and the "naughtiest night life".
Hamburg did not discover the Beatles alone, but a certain cool style of life. It is a cocktail of
seafaring romance and a fresh north-west breeze, exclusive elegance and classical tradition.
But it is also the gateway to the great seaside holiday area, the jumping-off point for tourist
high life in Westerland or Travemunde, or to a restful island holiday among the biggest
sand-tables of Old Germany.

It is again no great distance from Frankfurt to Munich, the world city with a heart,
the Olympic venue for 1972. Munich is Stimmung and the Hofbrauhaus, continuous
rejoicing and the Oktoberfest. Its great art gallery, the "Alte Pinakothek," provides a rendez-
vous with Rembrandt, Titian, Dürer and Raphael; and in the Schwabing district one meets
art and the artists in the street together. Here too is the home of cabaret and of the cheeky
chanson, the debating society and the elegant boutique. It is only a short hop to the Alps
with their jagged summits around the Zugspitze and Watzmann, their crystal-clear
mountain lakes, ski runs and sunny meadows.

Half-way between Frankfurt and Munich lies Baden-Baden, which can be taken here
as the representative of the many spas in the great complex of health resorts that is Germany.
In Baden-Baden the elegant world of Europe make a tryst year after year. The town is more
than just a watering-place. Here one makes a virtue of sickness, and conversation in the
well-groomed parks switches from circulatory troubles to international politics and back
again. And from here too, as from Stuttgart and almost any of Germany's populous cities,
it is no great distance to a typical German holiday area, in this case the Black Forest, the most
attractive of the many medium-altitude mountain areas between the Alps and the North Sea.

The natural park landscape is protected and – if damaged by attacks of any kind – restored
and maintained. 57 natural parks in the Federal Republic, with a total area of 4.5 million hectares,
are the result of the twenty-year-old natural park program. The idea of a united Europe has been
pursued in the founding of international "Europa Parks". Up to the present time, German-
Luxemburgian, German-Belgian, and, most recently, German-Dutch natural parks exist.

There is no denying it: Germany is Europe writ small – self-willed and charming at
the same time, bustling and dreamy, elegant and solid, ideal for all temperaments,
for those who travel in style as for those who travel light, for discoverers and aesthetes, for
artchasers and bikini-fanciers, for romantics and realists.

Romantische Dorf-Idylle
Drackenstein auf der
Schwäbischen Alb

Drackenstein is a romantic
village in the hills of the
Schwäbische Alb

Le village de Drackenstein,
une idylle romantique
dans les collines de la
Schwäbische Alb

El pueblo de Drackenstein,
un idilio romantico en las
colinas de la Schwäbische
Alb

The Germans, so people say, are not deflected from their path at work. They always have a goal before their eyes: a big car, a colour TV set, a new suite of furniture for the living room or even a little house with a garden around it, where roses and cauliflowers grow. And for this they keep on working, if need be far into the night. They make their place of work a second home: they build themselves, in the anonymity of the mass society, an oasis of individuality. Nearly every secretary looks after her office geranium with the same loving care as her typewriter; and at times the boss has his family in silver frames on his desk. Plush mascots sit on the workshop benches, and on many a hall-door, a horseshoe hangs to bring luck. Such "humus for the soul" is, according to psychologists, helpful to performance, and contributes to the "set fair" situation in the industrial climate. And it is only a permanent ridge of high pressure that can keep for the Federal Republic the leading position in the world economy, for which she is envied today.

Whether we think of Siemens or of Mannesmann, Klöckner, or of Bayer, the history of German firms is often as charged with tension as a Hitchcock thriller. About a century ago, shirt-sleeved pioneers, with the spirit of entrepreneurial adventure, unfailing flair for future prospects and a healthy attitude to money laid the bases of the concerns which today send their products out to the remotest corners of our earth. Today nine million men and women are working in 99,300 industrial enterprises: mechanical and electrical engineering, motor manufacturing, chemical industries and the textile trade are among the leading branches of our industrial hierarchy.

Since 1962 industrial output in the Federal Republic has risen by over 50%, and out of a 528,900 million mark turnover, more than 102,000 million mark were the share of exports. The label "made in Germany" has thus lost none of its commercial appeal, in spite of every criticism and even though competitors have appeared throughout the world, and particularly in Japan, causing many additional worries for our captains of industry.

When Herr Benz built his first car and Herr Thyssen lit his first blast furnace, almost half the German people earned their living on the land. Today they are scarcely ten per cent. The industrial revolution has transformed many structures and is transforming them further. Let us take another example. Ten years ago, along the Rhine, the Ruhr and the Saar, 150,000 miners spend their working hours underground. Today they are no more than 75,000. Coal has indeed come off second best in the battle with the world champion, oil, but no miner has had to tighten his belt to any significant extent as a result. The market economy in our State has always got back into balance up till now.

22.5 million workers, employees and executives go through office doors and factory gates every morning. And yet this legion of the industrious is not enough to satisfy the boom on the labour market. The State has therefore opened its frontiers, allowing Italians and Turks, Spaniards and Greeks into the country, to fill the gaps along the assembly lines and in the workshops. They are officially called "guest workers", but in reality the industrial process has naturalised them at least socially. The great building sites are a melting pot of the nations. All work together for our prosperity, and themselves partake of it.

And yet without Colleague Computer the race for the golden calf of affluence would have been lost. It is through his cooperation in the first instance that we have achieved the rationalisation which has raised productivity per worker by more than 50 per cent inside 10 years.

The "German economic miracle" – admired all over the world – has also been able to survive the recession of the past few years relatively well. Yet it would not have been possible without the excellent traffic network which exists in the Federal Republic. On the roads, rails, waters, in the air – everywhere life pulsates, it whirls and teems, and still one is able to reach one's destination with no great detours. Competition among the various individual transportation carriers has led to a standard which is simply wonderful. And this is true despite the fact that every weekend millions of Germany complain that their excursions have to end in bumper-to-bumper tie-ups.

In looking at these impressive statistical landmarks, we must not forget Gustav Schultze, the factory worker, who grows horny hands at his task in Wanne-Eickel, Frankfurt-Höchst or Stuttgart-Untertürkheim, who identifies himself personally with "his outfit", who points his children in the same way and who sees his dearest wish fulfilled when his daughter is promoted from assembly line to office. And who hangs up the testimonial, given to him by his firm for 25 or even 40 years' loyal service, like an expensive portrait over the sofa in the front room.

Men like Gustav Schultze, whose rights in the industrial process are being made increasingly secure by our free trade unions, are the guarantors of "Made in Germany". Fortunately, in our bustling and restless society, there are still a vast number of them.

For generations our people have applied themselves to the task of coping with progress. The Cassandras were always there. Yet, if the machine-breakers of the last centuries had been able to stop the wheel of time, there would be no 40-hour week today, no regular holidays, no jet trips to Majorca, and our womenfolk would still be careworn slaves at the cooking stove and the washing trough. Progress has given us all greater freedom, independence and self-confidence. And so long as the risk remains calculable, so long as reason sits in the brakesman's cabin of the express of the future, entries on the credit side will predominate in our balance-sheet. Thus we can see that the law which is to protect our environment is a very necessary pebble in the great mosaic of the future.

Whenever men have dared to venture one foot into the unexplored no-man's-land of the future there were Germans among them. We emerged from the "good old times" with the motorcar. The most commonly used types of engine bear German names. August Nikolaus Otto invented the first combustion engine, Karl Benz built the first petroldriven car and Rudolf Diesel made the engine named after him, which took advantage of cheap heavy oil as an economic source of power. Finally, Felix Wankel built the first rotary piston engine, whose future is only just beginning.

A few names, taken at random from the rollcall of those who have altered the face of our world, will make our contribution clear. There is Professor Werner Forssman whose heart catheter, in 1929, made decisive facts available for the general diagnosis of heart conditions. It was only much later, in 1965, that his pioneering deed was rewarded with the Nobel Prize. Then there is Karl Ferdinand Braun, the inventor of the tubes without which there could be no television. Far better known is Wernher von Braun, who gave, in America, the decisive impulse to the conquest of the moon. For generations progress has been linked with physicists – with Albert Einstein and his theory of relativity, with Max Planck and his quantum theory, with the first to split the atom, Professors Otto Hahn, Hugo Strassmann and Liese Meitner. In 1961 young Professor Rudolf Mössbauer won the Nobel Prize for his discovery of the energy structure of the atomic nucleus.

The Volkswagen has made progress in Germany an adventure. 1972 the Beetle, with 15 million cars, broke the production record of Ford's legendary "Tin Lizzie". Perhaps we should mention Leica, the miniature camera, which enlarged our photographic view of the world, and, very recently, the Effelsberg radio-telescope in the Eifel, the biggest ear in the world, which reaches out into the infinity of space to 100 trillion kilometres (that is, 10,000 million light years). Such superlatives reduce the other pioneering deeds of progress to the level of everyday routine. Then one takes for granted the closest motorway network in Europe, the densest television and telephone grid in the Old World, the highest ratio of car ownership and all the other visible signs which show us the future with their blessings and their problems.

Twenty-five years since the war have been enough to work a radical change in our view of the world. The German citizen, researched by opinion pollsters down to the last recess of his innermost feelings, has become self-confident; our Basic Law has done away with subjection, and with the obedient subject. As regards his propensity to travel, for instance, German Michael has become a citizen of the world, for whom the jump over the national frontier has become a joyous custom, and who proudly shows friends and relations his miniature film of the Pyramids or his slides from the Lake of Garda.

Increasing automation has been steadily reducing hours of work and lengthening free time and holidays. The highly developed industrial society has thus become, at the same time and as a logical consequence, a fastidious leisure society. On an average, 15 per cent of incomes now flow, as sociologists put it, into leisure consumption. Meanwhile whole industries concern themselves with the leisure-time activities of the people, and cities and municipalities make leisure facilities a standard feature of community planning. Thus the motor car has become the German's favourite toy. Prestige values are expressed in horse-power figures and, in order to burnish chrome and enamel to an ever-brighter gloss, a large part of the nation is to be found every Saturday in the street, performing with hose and polishing-rag the ritual cleansing of the first and foremost idol of general prosperity.

In their motorised conquest of leisure, the Germans have discovered their affinity for water: in gravel-pits and submerged quarries they have found a previously inaccessible world with possibilities for swimming and boating. And, throughout the country, cities and municipalities cooperate with leisure-time enthusiasts in the improvement of these lakes. Thus a circle is closed once again. Quite unobtrusively, out of what was a dreary landscape, an attractive oasis is created, with the smell of sausages and the laughter of children. The enthusiasts are even going one step further; there is talk in Parliament of how dumps and rubbish tips could be tidied up so as to become an attraction on the holiday programme.

During the week, of course, television determines the time-table as before. From eight o'clock the front room becomes a grandstand view on world affairs, and this all the more since the news commentator and the showgirl come into the house in colour. But there are two things even television cannot impair – the enjoyment of social life and the love of forming association. For many, the bar remains their favourite forum when work is over. Between two beers and a glass of schnapps, or several, people at the inn discuss as ever foreign policy, football results, holiday plans and their daily troubles.

Whole cities put on fancy dress, as disciplined office workers turn into an amusing crowd of clowns, pirates, gypsies and belly-dancers: everywhere, at some stage, there is always a local festival: the Oktoberfest in Munich – the greatest beer-drinking festival in the world – works on foreigners like a Bavarian natural phenomenon. And there is an occasion for collective rejoicing in nearly every village and every town throughout the year.

The shooting club has its celebration; the anniversary of the town charter must be commemorated; the fire brigade holds its gala; the church consecration festival brings the young people into the beer marquee; people meet to dance for the harvest home, the wine festival, the sausage market or the costume festival. At the head of the programme, however, stand the great galas. Kiel Week is one of them, with its international regattas; so are the drama festivals and great balls where people go to see and be seen.

People say that wherever two Germans meet they set up an association. This whimsical exaggeration caricatures a German national trait. Even popular hobbies are given an organised framework. And thus nowhere else in the world do people sing, dance, play skittles and potter about in officially constituted bodies as they do in our country. Stamp collectors and canary fanciers, model railway enthusiasts and skat players, ramblers and entomologists, nudists and expert cooks are proud to have their president and their articles of association. From all this, incidentally, women are no longer excluded. Emancipation has also asseted itself through leisure.

Perhaps we should also say a word about football. It is the biggest crowd-puller in this country. And with three million members the German Football Association is the largest sporting body in the world. At the weekend, stadiums are often crowded out, and the stars of the turf are honoured as once were the great idols of the screen. But whether football fan or weekend rambler, almost the whole of the nation has succeeded in making the most of its leisure, and in enjoying it.

Culture in Germany: that is like a ride on a great lift through all the floors of history. Gods and Ancient Germans, Romans and Barbarians, Emperors and Electors; Luther's Reformation; Gothic and Romanesque architecture; the Renaissance, the Jugendstil, the Bauhaus and the avant-garde of today.

Our many festivals have their roots deep in the past. Everywhere in the Federal Republic, even in the smallest village, one finds at least once a year some cause for rejoicing together. The Carnival on the Rhine and Fasching in the South are among the best-known occasions for merry-making, and their origins are to be found in past centuries.

One needs no set programme to go on a cultural tour of Germany. Whatever letter of the alphabet one hits upon in the gazetteer, art and culture are guaranteed. In this country, every age has carved its initials in stone. Towns such as Goslar, Rothenburg or Dinkelsbühl seem like the backdrop of a historical play, and many a smalltown market place could be taken for a medieval puppet show. But these things do not stand as dead memorials; they are brimful of life. And to give but one figure; in this country there are 150 specialist museums, dedicated to a variety of themes: old mail carriages, playing cards, bread, clocks and jewellery, leather. After the world famous galleries of ancient and modern art in Munich, Frankfurt, Nuremberg, Cologne, Hamburg, Bremen or Berlin, came the more recent art museums. Collections of ancient splendour beside contemporary avant-garde. Dürer next to Picasso, Marc Chagall beside Roy Lichtenstein – and they are only dots in the great mosaic of immortality. Nor should we forget the "Documenta" in Kassel – the world display of the moderns, who show us here how near we already stand to the year 2000.

Churches and cathedrals, many of which have endured for centuries while others took centuries to build, stand as the stone witnesses of culture and tradition. They tell of an age when they were the focus of learning and of art. Today, universities and academies have largely taken over their heritage, uniting teacher and taught in the search for knowledge and education.

If the Germans had to carry the burden which our contribution to the cultural development of the world imposed on them, they would all stubble along with aching backs under its weight. What Bach and Beethoven, Wagner, Schumann and Schubert, Haendel and Offenbach wrote in their note-sheets is in no danger of turning yellow in mothballs in the next hundred years. Festivals such as those in Bayreuth attract the music-loving élite of the whole world in evening dress. But the musical avantgarde has taken an irreverent stand, interpreted through Henze or Stockhausen. For in every tradition, and on the stage too, the great names do not overawe posterity. The theatre has shaken off the dust of time. Classics and moderns wage no fratricidal war. The operetta competes with the musical, politically committed groups are also allowed in the noble festival halls. There are 170 theatres in this country, with 130,000 seats together. And they put on a performance nearly every night. State and municipalities have dug deep in their coffers to provide all these seats in our temples of the muses, and private patrons have given them generous help.

The Federal Republic of Germany has culture for all. Of course it is not every town that has its own theatre company or orchestra. Hence the great and little stars are travellers as they always were. Jets and the Trans-Europe-Express have replaced the troupers' carriages; but as a long-established tournée land, we have an international reputation; and that is true of all branches of the "Culture business" throughout the year. When theatre or ballet companies, the ancients of jazz, folk, blues and gospel singers or the modern pop "bards" tramp through the land, even exhibition halls often become the festival halls of cultural consumption.

In the "things of culture", the Germans behaved as if they had sworn eternal loyalty to Goethe or Schiller on his deathbed. Even the television addict sometimes leaves the comfortable armchair of his bedroom cinema for the big platform. It is only in this way that one can explain how this country has a full house for the arts nearly every night.

S- und U-Bahnen ent-
lasten den Stadtverkehr
_____
Suburban trains and
subway systems make
city traffic easier

Le réseau urbain et le
métro dégage la
circulation automobile
au sein des villes
_____
El metro descongestiona
el tráfico urbano.

Intercity-Züge,
schnell und bequem

Inter-City Trains,
fast and comfortable

Trains intercity, rapides
et confortables

Los trenes "Intercity",
rápidos y cómodos.

≫

Wer zählt die Lichter,
nennt die Schiffe? Bremer
Häfen bei Nacht

Ships in the night: a view of
the harbour of Bremen

Nocturne dans le port
de Brême

Luzes y naves: la noche en
el puerto de Bremen

Airport-Lichter:
Vor dem Start eines
Lufthansa-Jets

Airport illumination:
Before the take-off of a
Lufthansa jet

Les feux de l'aéroport:
Un jet de la Lufthansa
s'apprête à décoller

Luces en el aeropuerto:
un avión de reacción
de la Lufthansa antes de
despegar

Glas und Beton: Modernes Bürohochhaus der Stinnes Zentralverwaltung in Mühlheim (Ruhr)

Glass and concrete: The modern headquarters of the Stinnes company in a sky-scraper at Mülheim (Ruhr)

Verre et béton l'administration centrale de la société Stinnes s'est installée dans ce gratte-ciel moderne

Vidrio y hormigón: El rascacielo moderno de la administración de la compañia Stinnes en Mülheim (Ruhr)

Öl aus Kohle: Großversuchsanlage von RAG und Veba in Bottrop

Oil from coal: the pilot plant of the "RAG" and "Veba" companies at Bottrop

Quand le charbon devient essence: l'usine pilote de la «RAG» et de la «Veba» à Bottrop

El carbón transformado en petróleo: Fábrica pilote de la "RAG" y de la "Veba" en Bottrop

Das Gesicht des Bergmanns

Portrait of a coal-miner

Tête de mineur

Cara de minero

Elektronik im Vormarsch. Endmontage des Microcomputers ,,Alphatronic" (Triumph-Adler AG)

Electronics, the spearhead of technological progress: the final assemblage of the microcomputer "Alphatronic" at the "Triumph-Adler" Company

L'électronique progresse sans cesse. Voici l'assemblage final du micro-ordinateur «Alphatronic» dans les ateliers de la «Triumph-Adler AG»

La electrónica en progreso. Fase final de la fabricatión del microcomputer "Alphatronic" en los talleres de la Compañía "Triumph-Adler"

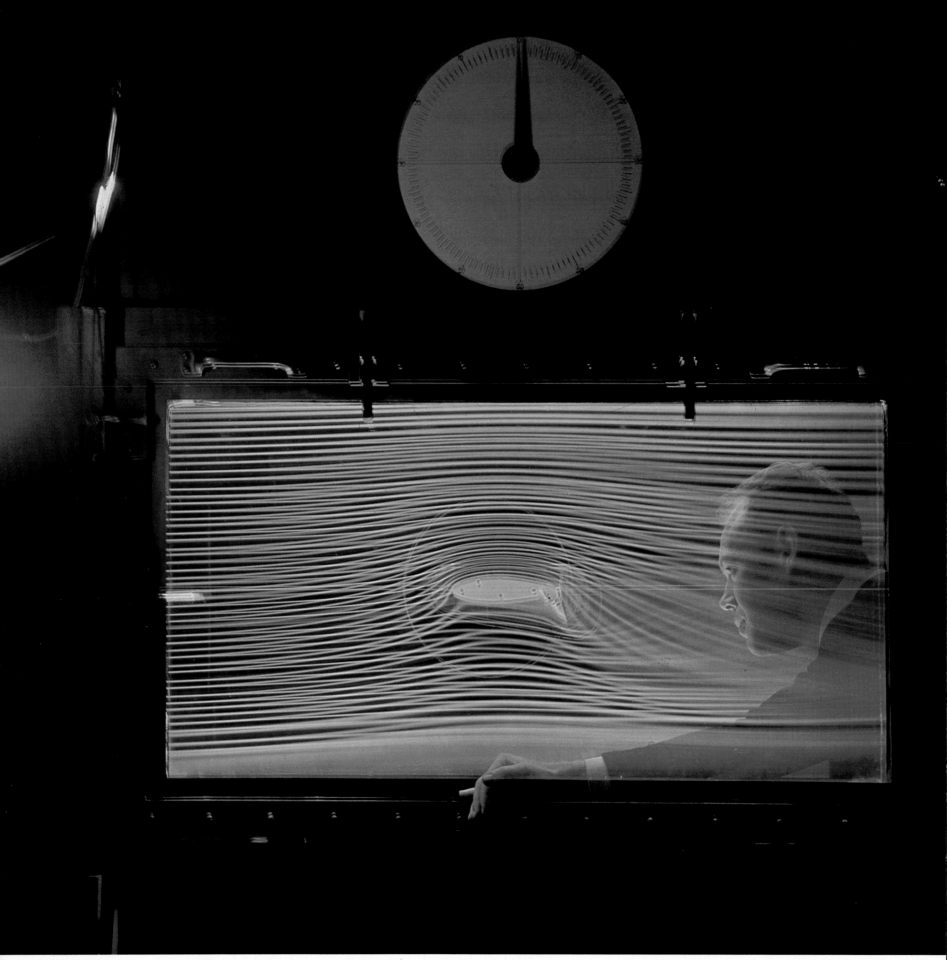

Wissenschaftler auf
neuen Wegen in der
Raumfahrttechnik

Scientists chart new
paths in space
technology

Les scientifiques à la
recherche de voies
nouvelles dans le
domaine de
l'astronautique

Científicos tras nuevos
derroteros en la técnica
de los viajes espaciales

Reihen-Versuche
in der Bayer-AG

Serial investigations
at Bayer AG

Séries d'essais chez Bayer

Ensayos en serie en la
Bayer-AG

Beispiele für zukunfts-
weisende Entwicklungen
von AEG Telefunken:
Solar-Generatoren zur
Direktstromerzeugung
und das schwebende Nah-
verkehrssystem M-Bahn

Two examples of promis-
ing technical developments
at the AEG Telefunken
works: A solar battery for
immediate power produc-
tion and the M-Bahn, a re-
volutionary short distance
transport system

Deux exemples de dé-
veloppements technolo-
giques prometteurs à la
société AEG Telefunken:
une génératrice pour la
production directe de
l'énergie solaire et le train

M-Bahn, un système révo-
lutionnaire pour les trans-
ports à courte distance

Ejemplos de un desarollo
técnico revolucionario en
las fábricas de la compañia
AEG-Telefunken: un ge-
nerador solar para la producción de energia electrica
directa y el treno M-Bahn,
un sistema ultramoderno
de comunicaciones urbanas

Die badischen Winzer
ganz modern: Ein
Großtankkeller

A Baden wine-cellar
full of large barrels

Les vignerons badois se
modernisent : une cave
pleine de grands fûts

Los viñeros badenses se
modernizan: gigantesca
bodega repleta de toneles

Produktion moderner
Einbauküchen bei
Poggenpohl, Herford

Manufacture of modern
fitted kitchens at
Poggenpohl in Herford

Poggenpohl, Herford :
Production de cuisines
fonctionnelles modernes

Producción de modernas
cocinas de tipo americano
estandardizadas, en la
casa Poggenpohl,
Herford

Satelliten-Funkstation
bei Raisting mit
Alpen-Panorama

Station satellite
près de Raisting et le
panorama alpin

Satellite radio station
near Raisting with
Alp panorama

Estación radiotelegráfica
por satélite cerca de
Raisting, con los Alpes
al fondo

Berliner „Milljöh"   Atmosphère berlinoise

Berlin "milieu"   «Ambientillo» berlinés

Fischmarkt im   Mercado de pescado de
Hamburger Hafen   Hamburgo

Fishmarket in the
port at Hamburg

Marché au poisson dans
le port de Hambourg

Olympia-Park
in München

Olympia Park
in Munich

Parc
olympique à Munich

Parque
Olímpico de Munich

Das ist Karneval! C'est cela le Carnaval!

This is carnival! Esto es el carnaval!

Beim Schützenfest in En el Festival de Tiro
Neuss en Neuss

Shooting festival in
Neuss

Fête des tireurs à Neuss

Boden-Turnerin

Gymnast

Gymnastique au sol

Gimnasia sueca

Auf dem Baldeney-See
in Essen

On the Baldeney-See in
Essen

Lac de Baldeney à Essen

Lago Baldeney en Essen

Die Augen offenhalten...
für's spätere Leben

Keep your eyes open ...
for later life

Savoir regarder autor de
soi . . . . . n'est jamais
temps perdu dans la vie

Mantener los ojos
abiertos . . . . . .
                para la vida
posterior

Im Grünen

Out in the country

Dans la verdure

En la foresta

Koblenz feiert
„Rhein in Flammen"

Koblenz celebrates
"Rhine in Flames"

Le «Rhin en flammes»
à Coblence

Coblenza festeja
«El Rin en Llamas»

Blick vom
Mannesmann-Hochhaus:
Düsseldorfer
Rhein-Romantik

View from the
Mannesmann tower
block: the romantic
Rhine at Düsseldorf

Vue de la tour
Mannesmann: le Rhin
romantique à Düsseldorf

Vista desde el rascacielos
Mannesmann:
Dusseldorf a orillas del
Rin

Radioteleskop Effelsberg
in der Eifel

Effelsberg radio
telescope in the Eifel

Radiotélescope à
Effelsberg dans l'Eifel

Radiotelescopio
Effelsberg en la región
de Eifel

Sonnen-Observatorium
Wendelstein

Solar observatory at
Wendelstein

Observatoire solaire à
Wendelstein

Observatorio solar en
Wendelstein

In der Spielbank
Bad Homburg
In the Casino
of Bad Homburg
Le casino
de Bad Hombourg

En el Casino
de Bad Homburg

Gruppenpädagogisches
Seminar gefördert vom
Deutsch-Französischen
Jugendwerk
Casual seminar conducted
by the German-French
Youth Organization

Séminaire sans contrainte
de l'Association Franco-
Allemande de la Jeunesse
Coloquio ameno en la
Organización Franco-
Alemana de la Juventud

Freude beim
sportlichen Fliegen:
50 000 Deutsche sind
dabei

Enjoying flying as a sport:
50,000 Germans take part

Les plaisirs du sport
aérien : 50.000 Allemands
s'y adonnent

50.000 alemanes son
aficionados al deporte
aéreo

≪ Galopp-Rennen

Racing

Courses au galop

Al galope

Rheinstadion
in Düsseldorf

Rhine Stadium
in Düsseldorf

Le stade du Rhin à
Düsseldorf (Rhein-
stadion)

El estadio del Rin
en Düsseldorf

Vergnügungs-Floßfahrt
auf der Isar

Pleasure raft on the Isar

Radeau de plaisance sur
l'Isar

Viaje de placer sobre
troncos a través del Isar

Im Wattenmeer

Mud-flats

Sur la plage à marée
basse

Marea baja en la playa

Oktoberfest in München
The Oktoberfest Munich
Fête d'octobre à Munich
Festival de Octubre en
Munich

Rennbahn in
Baden-Baden/Iffezheim

Art the edge
of the race-track in
Baden-Baden/Iffezheim

Au bord de la piste à
Baden-Baden/Iffezheim

Al borde de la pista de
carrera en
Baden-Baden/Iffezheim

In der Miniaturstadt „Minidomm" bei Düsseldorf

At "Minidomm", the miniature city near Düsseldorf

La ville miniature «Minidomm», près de Düsseldorf

En la ciudad en miniatura «Minidomm» cerca de Düsseldorf

Der Traum vom eigenen Häuschen – hier mit Hilfe der Kölner Bausparkasse Heimbau AG realisiert

The dream of an individual home – specialized savings banks like the "Kölner Bausparkasse Heimbau AG" help to make it come true

Le rêve d'une maison individuelle – Des caisses d'épargne spécialisées permettent de le réaliser, comme par exemple la «Kölner Bausparkasse Heimbau AG»

El sueño de la casita individual cajas de ahorro especializadas permiten de materializarlo como por ejemplo la "Kölner Bausparkasse Heimbau AG"

Die Nation ist gespannt: Jeden Samstag Ziehung der Lottozahlen

The country waits on tenterhooks: The Lotto numbers are drawn every Saturday night

Chaque samedi, la nation entière attend fièvreusement le tirage des numéros de lotto

La nación está impaciente: cada sábado hay sorteo

Schmuck aus vier Jahrtausenden: Schmuckmuseum Pforzheim

Four thousand years of jewellery:

"Schmuckmuseum" of Pforzheim

Bijoux provennants de quatre millenaires. Le musé des ornements de Pforzheim

Joyas de un período de cuatro mil años: Museo de joyas en Pforzheim

Im Theater zu
Wiesbaden

Wiesbaden theatre

Au théâtre à Wiesbaden

Teatro de Wiesbaden

Rokoko-Festsaal im
Augsburger
Schaezlerpalais

Rococo hall in the
Schaezler Palace,
Augsburg

Salle de fêtes de style
rococo dans le Palais
Schaezler d'Augsbourg

Salón Rococó en el
Palacio Schaezler en
Augsburgo

Bauernbett aus Bad Tölz

Country bed from Bad Tölz

Lit de paysan de Bad Tölz

Cama rústica de Bad Tölz

Museum in Baden-Baden

Museum in Baden-Baden

Musée à Baden-Baden

Museo en Baden-Baden

Lebendiges Museum:
Windenschmiede von
1745 bei J. D. Neuhaus
in Witten

Living museum:
Windeschmiede (wind
forge) of 1745 at
J. D. Neuhaus in Witten

Musée vivant: La forge
de treuils de la maison
S. D. Neuhaus, Witten,
datant de 1745

Museo con vida: fragua
de tornos de 1745 de
J. D. Neuhaus en Witten

Im Gutenberg-Museum
zu Mainz

In the Gutenberg
Museum in Mainz

Le musé de Gutenberg
à Mayence

En el museo de
Gutenberg en Mainz

Prozession in Seeon
(Chiemgau)
_____

Procession in Seeon
(Chiemgau)
_____

Procession à Seeon
(Chiemgau)

Procesión en Seeon
(Chiemgau)

Triumph-Kreuz (1230) im
Dom zu Osnabrück
_____

Triumphal cross (1230) in
Osnabrück cathedral
_____

Croix triomphale (1230)
dans la Cathédrale
d'Osnabrück

Cruz trifunal (1230) en la
Catedral de Osnabrück

Hier im Friedenssaal
zu Münster endete der
Dreißigjährige Krieg

The Thirty Years' War
was ended here in the
Friedenssaal in Münster

Le traîté, signé, ici, dans
la «Salle de la Paix» de
Munster, mettait fin a la
Guerre de Trente Ans.

Aquí, en la Sala de la
Paz de Münster, terminó
la Guerra de los
Treinta Años.

Der Fastnachtbrunnen
in Mainz

The Fastnachtbrunnen
in Mainz

La fontaine du carnaval
à Mayence

La fuente
«Fastnachtbrunnen»
en Mainz

Szene aus der
„Zauberflöte"
Staatsoper München

Scène de la «Flûte
enchantée» de Mozart —
Opéra d'Etat de Munich

Ballett in der Deutschen
Oper am Rhein
Duisburg/Düsseldorf

Ballet à l'Opéra allemand
sur le Rhin à Duisburg/
Düsseldorf

Scene from "The Magic
Flute" — Munich
State Opera

Escena de "La Flauta
Mágica" de Mozart
Opera del Estado de
Munich

Ballet at the German
Opera on the Rhine
Duisburg/Düsseldorf

Representación de
ballet en la Opera
Alemana del Rin
(Duisburg/Düsseldorf)

Staatsoper München:
Szene aus „Salome"

Munich State Opera:
Scene from "Salome"

L'Opéra d'Etat de
Munich: Scènes de
«Salomé»

Opera del Estado de
Munich Escena de
"Salome"

Isang Yun, „Träume" –
Opernaufführung in
Nürnberg

"Dreams",
by Isang Yun – opera
premiere in Nuremberg

«Rêves» d'Isang Yun –
Soirée d'opéra à
Nuremberg

Isang Yun "Sueños" –
función de ópera en
Nuremberg

Silberne Telleruhr/
17. Jahrh. Wuppertaler
Uhrenmuseum

17th century silver plate
clock, Wuppertal clock
museum

Assiette-horloge en   >
argent du 17ème
siècle — Musée de
l'horlogerie à Wuppertal

Plato-reloj del siglo
XVII Museo de
Relojería de Wuppertal